HOW TO READ OGHAM

*A practical guide to
Ogham Divination
from The Apophis Club*

by Orry Whitehand

A Publication of The Apophis Club

HOW TO READ OGHAM

Table of Contents

The Apophis Club Draconian Magic Series

APOPHIS
Ægishjálmur: The Book of Dragon Runes
Dragonscales
Draconian Consciousness
Words of Power
The Grimoire of the Sevenfold Serpent
Gods and Monsters
Runes of Mann
The Sevenfold Mystery (forthcoming)

The Apophis Club Practical Guide Series

How To Read Ogham
How to Conjure a Spirit (forthcoming)

What is the Apophis Club Practical Guides Series?

The Apophis Club Practical Guides Series is a new series of small booklets and ebooks intended to complement The Apophis Club's main range of Draconian titles.

Whereas the main range of titles are packed full of philosophical and initiatory speculation, this series of practical guides eschew all historical and philosophical musing and limit themselves exclusively to providing a simple, point by point instruction on how to work magic.

Each booklet will deal with a different subject, offering precise instruction as a 'how to' manual in that subject. The intention is that Club Initiates and other interested readers will be able to immediately gen up on magical practices they are currently unfamiliar with and put them to practical use. The philosophy behind such use can be found in the main range books. Thus, readers are able to expand their magical repertoire without constantly retreading the same theoretical material.

HOW TO READ OGHAM

Chapter One

What is Ogham Divination?

This little booklet aims to teach you how to read the Celtic ogham characters for the purpose of divination. It is a purely practical instruction manual, intent upon giving you the information you need in order to actually **do** something and put the principles into practice. As such, all historical or philosophical information is kept to a bare minimum, except that which is absolutely necessary for you to understand what you are doing. Once you have got the hang of actual **use** of ogham, you are welcome to read much more deeply in the books listed at the rear of this booklet if you so wish.

The booklet is divided into four sections:

- What the ogham letters are
- The meanings of the ogham
- How to make your own ogham set
- How to use the ogham for divination

In short, the booklet will instruct you in the shapes, sounds and values of the ogham; what they mean; how to make and charge a set, and how to use them to cast divinations (or, more colloquially, 'fortune telling').

The process of divination is a means of communication between the magician's consciousness and the collective unconscious, allowing the reader to discern the patterns unfolding in the world and offer advice about how best to proceed with a given project or problem.

In everyday communication, words are arranged in sentences in such a way to communicate the thoughts of the speaker. For example, "I am feeling tired" would communicate the idea that I would really prefer not to do anything active, but would like to sit down and rest or even go to bed. Each word has a meaning, and this meaning makes sense when it is combined with other words in a particular order

In ogham divination, the 'words' of our communication are the ogham letters (or 'fews' as they are called), and they are arranged according to a 'layout' which represents the structure of the sentence, defining the message they convey. The specific fews which fall in particular places in the layout are then read in conjunction with each other, allowing the reader to interpret an overall message in relation to the question which has been asked.

Chapter Two

What are the Ogham Letters?

The ogham letters are normally called 'fews' (from the Old Irish word *fidhe*). There are twenty 'standard' ogham fews, plus a further five later additions which represent the diphthongs and are not used in divination.[1] We will therefore focus our attention solely upon the original twenty fews which are used practically in divination.

The fews are arranged in four rows, each containing five fews. Each few has a stemline, and the group is determined by the position of the cross strokes which cross the line. The first group of fews have notches to the right of the stemline; the second group have notches to the left of the stemline; the third group

---

1   The additional five diphthong fews (called the *forfedha*) are taken to represent cosmic principles. As such, they actually form the basis for the fivefold layouts used in this booklet. Such cosmological and theoretical matters are discussed in detail in Michael Kelly's *The Book of Ogham* for those who are interested.

9

has strokes which cut diagonally across the stemline; the final group (the vowels) have strokes which cut straight across the stemline. The number of notches or strokes determine which few within a group is signified. Thus two notches to the right of the stemline ╞ signifies *luise*, the L-few, the second few in the first group.

The table below illustrates all four groups with the letter attributions:

BLFSN   HDTCQ

M G ng Z R   A O U E I

The 'feather mark' ➤ at the commencement of each group indicates the beginning of the line of text, and the order in which it should be read.

The names of these ogham fews in their proper sequence are tabulated below, together with the meanings of those names in Old Irish (which give clues to each few's esoteric meaning in divination):

B	*beithe*	"birch-tree"
L	*luise*	"flame, radiance" and *lus* "plant, herb, vegetable"
F	*fern*	"alder-tree"
S	*sail*	"willow-tree"
N	*nin*	"forked branch" and "lofty"
H	*úath*	"fear, horror"
D	*duir*	"oak-tree"
T	*tinne*	"bar, rod of metal, ingot, mass of molten metal"
C	*coll*	"hazel"

10

Q	*cert*	"bush" and "rag"
M	*muin*	"neck" and "trick" and "love"
G	*gort*	"field"
ng	*gétal*	"(act of) wounding, slaying"
Z	*straif*	"sulphur"
R	*ruise*	"reddening"
A	*ailm*	"pine-tree" (?)
O	*onn*	"ash-tree"
U	*úr, úir*	"earth, soil; grave"
E	*éo*	"salmon" > *edad* "aspen"
I	*éo*	"yew-tree" > *idad*

For practicality of use and to prevent confusion, the two final fews, E and I, are generally referred to by their alternate names of *edad* and *idad* rather than both being called *éo*.

HOW TO READ OGHAM

Chapter Two

What are the Ogham Meanings?

This chapter will provide divinatory meanings for each of the ogham fews in sequence and will finish with a chart cross-referencing key words for each few for the main fivefold layout which will follow in the next chapter.

├ B Beithe

Beithe is concerned with births, with beginnings of things. It is possessed of an enormous vitality which can be channeled into new projects and aspirations. These influences can range from the literal birth of a new family member, the arrival of a new but significant person or influence in your life, a new job / career, a change for the better in terms of health (that surge of vital energy inherent in the few), or a complete change in lifestyle and circumstances.

There is something intensely positive about *beithe*, and the changes and new beginnings with which

13

it deals will almost always be positive too, a dynamic and fun adventure for those with the spirit to enjoy such things. But this does not imply that the process will always be painless. Even the good fortune of *beithe* has its price.

Every change brings uncertainty, it involves the removal of the old and comfortable as well as the introduction of the new and exciting. It can involve loss and uncertainty, a lack of security for an indeterminate period of time.

The best way to approach the spirit of *beithe* is with an open mind and a sense of adventure, an intense curiosity about the larger world beyond your current horizons. Such an attitude will never fail to be rewarded by the current of *beithe*.

⊨ L   Luise

The **L**-few indicates that there exists within you a deep spring of insight and understanding that can be tapped to assist you in life. Its lesson is that no matter how bleak or negative your situation appears to be, the keys to its solution are to be found in the deep places of your own soul, if you can only reach for them.

This insight is also useful in seeing the motivations of others clearly, and ensuring that you are not being manipulated or unduly influenced. It can also require a lot of courage sometimes to act upon your own inner conviction, contrary to the concerted opinion of those others around you.

╞ F Fern

The qualities contained within *fern* incorporate such aspects as steadfastness, integrity and objective knowledge. The few implies, or encourages, the discovery of underlying principles deep beneath the surface soap opera which surrounds any given situation. *Fern* goes directly to the root of a problem.

The **F**-few also emphasises the discovery of the founding principles within one's own self, the numinous apprehension of such questions as, "Who am I?", "What am I?", "Why am I?" One's inner foundation is contextual to one's circumstances in life. As these change and greater life experience is won, so the very core of self experiences a maturation and a greater coming into being.

╞ S Sail

Sail deals with undercurrents, with those things which pass beneath the surface of observable everyday life, but which nonetheless influence its course.

Sail refers to the powers of the imagination. It promotes the development of psychic abilities and can be used to enhance the recall of dreams, or dream work in general.

╞ N Nin

Nin represents true visionary abilities, always seeing the larger picture and discerning the truth behind surface appearances.

The cosmic balance of this few is indicative of its

15

twin meanings: peace and rebirth. At first glance, these two appear contradictory, as peace is a passive state of being, whereas rebirth is intensely active. In truth, they are the two poles of a single process, harmonised in *nin*. The fivefold patterning of the few signifies the end of one cycle of being and the commencement of another.

⊣ H Úath

The **H**-few generally implies disruption in the ordinary affairs of life. It may involve a streak of bad luck, it may involve intentional malice against you from some source. The message underlying these symptoms is generally the same: step back, take stock of your life, identify what is necessary, then move on.

This misfortune may come from within as well as from without. You may be secretly sabotaging yourself because you inwardly realise that you are making no headway and that it is time for a change, a re-evaluation of your life. In such a case, the best course of action is to stop, take time out to think, set your life in order. Then, and only then, is the time to move on.

The unpleasantness associated with *úath* is always a warning that it is time to pause and check the direction and purpose of your life.

⊣ D Duir

The primary meaning of *duir* is one of strength, courage and endurance. It is the courage to be true to one's most fundamental principles in the face of all opposition, to stand as steadfast and proud as an old oak in the face of the storm. There is a deep honour

16

and heroism about the few.

Great knowledge and wisdom is also associated with *duir*, as befits its strong links with the druids. There is a sense of great age about this few, and those who can apprehend its essence can gaze both backwards and forwards through the mists of time to discern the patterns of unfolding events. *Duir* is a boundary between realms, between the past and the future, as well as between this world, the Underworld and the Otherworld.

⊟ T Tinne

At its best, *tinne* is indicative of a directed balance, the ability to weigh all sides of a question and decide upon a proportionate response which will best further one's goals in the light of the circumstances. It also signifies justice and retribution for wrong-doing, and carries a sense of honour and duty.

⊟ C Coll

Coll represents the entire creative impulse and the ability to work with it and express it. As such, it has three aspects:
1. The ability to see beyond the mere outer shape of a thing or an idea, perceiving its innermost essence, those rarefied qualities which truly make it what it is. This is the aspect of recognition.
2. The ability to perceive new and wonderful ways in which these qualities may be expressed and manipulated. This is the aspect of creativity.
3. The application of due skill and mastery in your craft

to express these essential qualities in ways in which they can be appreciated by other people, and can move them in the way you intended. This is the aspect of work.

Through exercise of the qualities of this few, you can learn to apply its principles in all of life's situations, and can bring creative and inspiring solutions to bear upon many human problems, simply by mixing the essential qualities of the situation in new and refreshing ways. Ultimately, life becomes a wonderful and stimulating game.

≣ Q Cert

The primary meaning of *cert* is to seek after beauty and proportion in all things. The thrust of this idea is something a little strange to modern minds, where beauty is perceived as something passive to be admired, instead of something active to be aspired towards.

This is perhaps made clearer when considering the ogham's links with eternity. In his *Symposium*, Plato made a strong argument for a link between the principles of beauty and eternity. True beauty, in order to be fully beautiful, must also by definition be immortal, otherwise its beauty is spoiled. Seeking after beauty therefore transmutes into the quest for immortality.

┼ M Muin

Muin represents the intertwining of the conscious and subconscious strata of the psyche, allowing a deeper and much more complex perspective on life.

The process is a gentle and cumulative one. Logic and rational thought are not cast out, but instead are gradually supplemented with intuition and inspiration. It is an extension of one's limits into new areas, a new experience of the interplay between inner and outer, upper and lower.

⊬ G Gort

Gort is the principle of transformation from a base condition to a higher state. It is exemplified by fine craftsmanship, which uses the application of the focused will, the proper tools, and hard won skills over a period of time to painstakingly create items of intricate beauty and value.

As such, the few corresponds with any attempts to use one's skills to move the tone of a given situation from a lower level to a higher. It is the ability to make the most of the tools and the position at hand to create something perfect and satisfying.

⊯ ng Gétal

Gétal recognises that the subjective world within and the objective world without, while distinct from one another, nevertheless may influence one another, and that the querent can learn from both.

This is quite distinct from the meaning of *muin*, which stresses the intertwinings between conscious and subconscious levels of the psyche, and the interactions between self and not-self. *Gétal* instead seeks to harmonise them and synchronise the inner and outer worlds, making them run in parallel, whilst recognising the two as separate continua.

≢ Z Straif

Straif refers to those powers which control and constrain us which have their origin outside of ourselves. More often than not, this is a negative force, limiting personal freedom and choice. Certainly, whenever the few falls in a divinatory context, it can always be assumed to refer to such a scenario, with the querent being controlled – very possibly without even realising it – and persuaded to follow somebody else's agenda instead of following his/her own path.

Very often, the main key in transforming a situation involving *straif* is simply to become aware of its influence and to identify the controlling force. Once recognised, its insidious power is lost and it can be resisted and made allowance for, or – sometimes – even accepted and worked with consciously, on your own terms. In such a case, the element of choice is restored to the querent.

≣ R Ruise

Ruise is the realisation that all things change. The world around us changes, people are born and die, new things are made and old things break apart. Even our own bodies are completely replaced on a cellular level every few years.

The mental trauma many people feel with this few is that we become attached to familiar things and are afraid of having to accustom ourselves to new things. But it is inevitable that life is full of such changes. We cannot remain a child, we grow up. Play is left behind, we must be educated. School is left behind, we must work. Marriage and children follow, then retirement and death. Life follows its inexorable cycle, and within these greater cycles, the smaller, more personal, wheels of fate are turning.

The question of *ruise* is whether we are swept along by these cycles from crisis to crisis, or whether we make use of them to enrich life. Every change in life is an opportunity for new knowledge, achievement and joy. Every challenge thrown down is a new victory to be won. There is no point in fighting the inevitable, but you can liberate yourself from tyranny by using changes in your environment and circumstances to explore and express yourself more fully, in ways that may have been inappropriate or impossible previously. Life can be play.

We must come to terms with the changing world and assume responsibility for our own responses to, and uses of, it.

✝ A Ailm

The **A**-few implies that an objective eye is used to establish boundaries and to order the world around you into a coherent and productive one. This process of bringing order to a chaotic cosmos is the first step on the path of enlightenment. Where once chaos reigned the sovereign will imposes discipline and a sense of priorities.

The true sovereign here, of course, is the individual psyche, which must bring order to its own world, as each human being who wishes to be successful in life must take steps to introduce order and cohesion. It is not enough to be tossed and bruised by chance factors in life, it is necessary to take control and to introduce measures for dealing with life and actively taking control of it and steering where you want it to go. This is a very demanding task, which is why it is compared with the task of kings.

In a divinatory context, the appearance of this few might signify that some new responsibility and opportunity may present itself to the querent. As such, it is a warning to act with forethought and due consideration.

ⵜ O Onn

Onn represents the attainment of wisdom by the ingathering and synthesis of valuable and pertinent things. One of the other symbols for this few is the beehive, for honey is a sweet substance which is the result of hard work and gathering by bees.

Most particularly in a divinatory context, the few refers to drawing together all of the different strands of your life and deliberately dedicating them to your chosen goal. In this way, wisdom is won and all of your resources work together instead of pulling in different directions. Wisdom is a numinous quality which is only attained when a certain quantity and quality of work has been done previously, allowing a firm foundation from which intuition may spring.

ⵜ U Ur

Ur encompasses all aspects of passion, including the dreamy and romantic. There is a fire within it too, however, for when a subject is aflame with passion, the conscious and subconscious levels of the psyche become united as one in their desire. Passion acts as a vivifying and unifying force upon consciousness and it is in this way that it becomes a gateway, firstly to inner realms of the self but also to new opportunities in life.

When this few appears in a divinatory reading, or is used in a magical process, it is usually a call to open up sufficient room for passion to manifest in life, so that the querent may truly live and cease merely existing. This is a vivacious few.

≢ E Edad

There is a dynamic polarity inherent within the E-few. On the one hand, it signifies negative or turbulent situations arising which may threaten to overwhelm the querent. On the other hand, it promises that the querent may overcome all of these challenges by drawing upon inner reserves of strength and heroism.

It is a fact that if we do not have difficult and troublesome situations in life against which to test our mettle, these inner strengths are never sought out and put into practice, and we simply stagnate, stuck in a rut. How many people do you know who fit this model, whose lives have led nowhere for years, because they have always considered it prudent to back down in the face of challenges, to take the easy route? There will always be resistance to progress; the comfortable old will resist the incursions of the unknown new. Sometimes this resistance will be internal, a struggle against our own idleness or habits, sometimes it will be external as our peers insist that a new and revolutionary idea should be forgotten. It takes courage to struggle on, often alone, but to the victor the spoils.

≣ I Idad

The primary meaning of this few is that of transformation, a total change in circumstances. The most extreme example of this type of change – and the underlying meaning of the few – is obviously that of death. In a divinatory context, however, when this ogham falls in a significant place, it will most often point to a major upheaval and/or crisis in that aspect of life to which the divination refers. This could refer to a change in job, location or personal relationships. It marks the end of one state of being and the transition to a new, different one. As such, it may infer a certain amount of discomfort and trauma if the change is unwanted or unexpected.

In a metaphysical sense, the few does not only refer to death itself, but also to that which survives, which possesses continuity to transfer over from one state of being to the next. As such, it touches right to the core of the soul, to the root principles that make us what we are. It is a key to discovering those things within which are eternal and abiding and which may make the transition from life through death into life.

The main challenge of this ogham is that of overcoming the sense of loss and grief which always accompanies such traumatic change. When the old and familiar is swept irrevocably away, it can be difficult in the extreme to let it go. But until this is done, the potential of the new situation cannot be addressed and enjoyed.

24

Chart of Key Words

In the chapter on reading ogham, the primary layout has five fields in which the ogham fews are placed, these fields being labeled respectively Sovereignty, Harmony, Learning, Conflict and Prosperity (this will become clearer in due course, when the actual method of reading is explained.)

These fields obviously adapt and influence the meanings of the fews that are placed in them. For example, the eighteenth few, *Ur* ≡ meaning passion, will have a very different emphasis and interpretation if it lands in the field of Harmony than if it lands in the field of Conflict. Harmony is a peaceful state, which can be disrupted by passion; conflict is a stressful state, in which passion can lead to courage and victory. This shows how an ogham can be either positive or negative depending upon its placement (plus its relationship with the other fews in a reading).

To make this easier for new readers, I have formulated a table below which signifies a key word for each ogham few in each of the fields of a fivefold layout. This should give a little helping hand to initial interpretation of a reading.

Few	Sound	Sovereignty	Harmony	Learning	Conflict	Prosperity
├	B	Mead	Disturbance	Eagerness	Fury	Riches
⊨	L	Dominion	Craft	Discovery	Cunning	Abundance
⊫	F	Principles	Quickness	Laziness	Vigilance	Obstruction

HOW TO READ OGHAM

Few	Sound	Sovereignty	Harmony	Learning	Conflict	Prosperity
ᚄ	S	Insight	Subtlety	Cunning	Advantage	Loathing
ᚅ	N	Renewal	Tyranny	Satisfaction	Affluence	Poverty
ᚆ	H	Weakness	Disharmony	Ignorance	Defeat	Poverty
ᚇ	D	Realisation	Discontent	Recognition	Destruction	Rest
ᚈ	T	Steadfast	Rejection	Judgement	Vengeance	Preparation
ᚉ	C	Eloquence	Beauty	Teaching	Arbitration	Arts
ᚊ	Q	Perfection	Satisfaction	Esoterica	Doubt	Completion
ᚋ	M	Dignity	Subtlety	Modesty	Pride	Prestige
ᚌ	G	Developm't	Entertainm't	Education	Ruin	Futility
ᚍ	ng	Stability	Harmony	Beauty	Rest	Manners
ᚎ	Z	Steward	Vehemence	Testing	Capture	Debt
ᚏ	R	Maturity	Knowledge	Advancem't	Survival	Generosity
ᚐ	A	Sovereignty	Discovery	Mastery	Strategy	Originality
ᚑ	O	Guidance	Rulership	Passion	Change	Security
ᚒ	U	Inspiration	Disturbance	Eagerness	Fury	Greed
ᚓ	E	Overcoming	Completion	Discipline	Force	Craft
ᚔ	I	Transform	Discord	Disillusion	Fear	Loss/Grief

Chapter Three

Making Your Ogham Set

Before you begin reading the ogham, you will need to make your own set of the twenty fews. This can be done quite easily.

Ideally, you will want to make your fews from wood. You can either cut your own slices of wood from a small branch, sanding them down to size, or you can buy a set of craft sticks (iced lolly sticks) and use these pre-prepared ones.

If you're really keen to start immediately and don't want to have to wait till you've made a proper wooden set, you could always draw the fews onto blank cards with a red marker pen as a temporary measure, but you should fashion your own wooden set as soon as possible. They really will repay the effort you put into them, forming a stronger connection with you every time they are used.

The first step is to cut one ogham few into each of the twenty pieces, using a craft knife, or perhaps tapping with a sharp, slim chisel if the pieces of wood

27

are chunky enough. The fews should be prepared in their proper order until all twenty are done.

Remember to make a feather mark ⟩- at the base of the few to indicate the direction in which it should be read. Otherwise, once they have been jumbled up, you won't know if ⊢ is a right way up *beithe* or an upside down *úath*. These two fews, for example, should look like this:

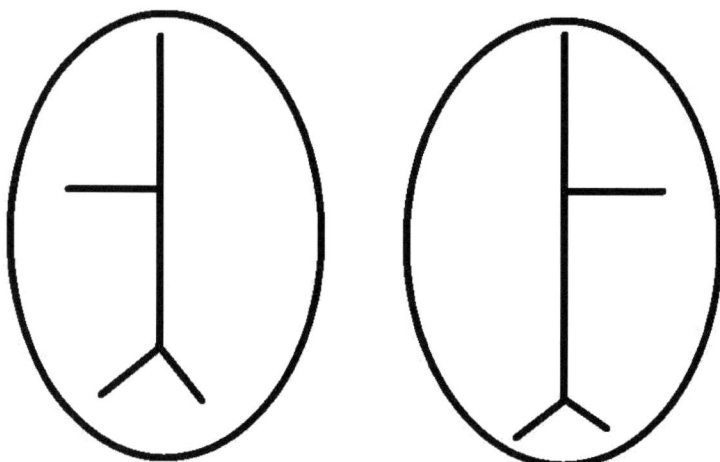

Úath   Beithe

Once the fews have been carved into the wood, they need to be coloured. Use a red ink or paint, the colour of life. You may wish to add just a drop of your own blood to further vivify the fews and connect them with yourself by a magical bond. This colour should be carefully applied within the grooves that have been cut in the wood, marking out the shape of the few.

Once the fews have been coloured and the paint has been allowed to dry, it is time to charge them for use. Place a bowl of water and a lit candle before you. Pick up each few in turn, in their proper order, and hold it close to your mouth. Chant its name, 'singing' it into the wood, bringing the ogham to life, concentrating hard all the while upon what the few means and signifies. When your concentration begins to wane, inhale deeply and breathe your hot breath 'into' the ogham, linking it to your own vitality.

Finally, take the few and sprinkle a little water upon it and pass it briefly through the candle flame. This will consecrate it and remove any influences but your own. This consecration can be repeated periodically to remove any psychic detritus the fews may accumulate from those you read for.

When all twenty fews have been charged and consecrated, they should be stored in a cloth bag and placed in a dry, dark place until they are needed for use.

HOW TO READ OGHAM

Chapter Four

Casting and Interpreting the Ogham

Before you begin an ogham reading, it is useful to carry out a ritual opening. This will serve to shut out workaday distractions and attune your to the task, focusing your mind upon the ogham fews and the question you wish to investigate.

Once the ritual opening has been completed, select the layout you wish to use for the reading and then begin. Be sure to record the positions of all fews that are laid out in the reading, plus your impressions at the time, so you will be able to refer back to these later. This will be an invaluable tool in learning from both your successful and erroneous interpretations, fine tuning your psychic receptivity to the ogham.

Ritual Opening

1. Face North, laying the bag of ogham fews upon the reading surface before you.
2. Hold your arms out at your sides in a cross-wise

posture and recite the following: *"Before me stands Ériu in Fal, on my right stands Nuada in Gor, on my left stands the Dagda in Mur, and at my back stands Lugh in Fin. May each bless me and go before me in all that I do here."* As you do so, visualise the four towering forms surrounding you: Ériu in the North is a richly dressed woman standing upon a great stone; Nuada in the East is a silver-handed king holding a spear; the Dagda in the West is a bearded, pot-bellied man wielding a great club and standing behind a cauldron; Lugh in the South is a radiant sun-king holding a sword.

3. Still facing North, hold your arms out before you and say: *"I call upon all the Gods and Goddesses on which my forebears called and swore their oaths. Come, be with me in all I do here. I call upon the Dagda, the Good God; upon Lugh, the Shining One; upon the strong Ogma; and upon Manannán of the Deep."*

4. Take up the bag of ogham fews in your cupped hands, hold them just beneath your mouth and say over them: *"I call upon you, the three Brigids, to guide my hands and the ogham fews. I call upon you, the three Morríghna, to guide my mind and the ogham fews that I might see and read in them what is right and true."*

5. Then reach into the bag, drawing out ogham fews and setting them down in your chosen layout.

6. Before commencing with interpreting the reading, raise your hands, covering your right eye with

your left hand and your left eye with your right hand. Let your mind enter a meditative state.

7. Now begin your interpretation, referring to the ogham meanings given in chapter two, combined with the layout meanings given in this chapter. The examples should help with this process, which will become much easier and more fluid with experience, when your communication with the inner oghams deepens.

8. Be sure to record everything.

9. Put the oghams back in their bag, reach out your arms before you and offer a brief thanks to the Gods and Goddesses of your ancestors for assisting you in interpreting the reading aright.

The Way of Brigid

This layout is a very simple one, suitable for beginners, but also useful for advanced readers when considering simple questions. Since it uses only three fews and three fields in which to lay them, the balancing and cross-referencing of meanings is not too complex.

There are three 'layers' to the Celtic cosmos: this world of matter in which we live; the Underworld, and the Otherworld.

The first few to be drawn from the bag is placed in the centre of the reading surface and represents the situation from the perspective of our everyday reality. The second few is placed a couple of inches beneath it, and represents the Underworld, and the hidden roots and formative influences of the situation. The third few is placed a couple of inches above the first one and represents the Otherworld, showing the potential for

33

transforming the situation.

Example Reading Using the Way of Brigid

A friend is besotted with a woman he works with. Finding it difficult to rein in his passion, he wants to know whether she feels the same, and whether he should make advances toward her. The oghams are mixed and three pulled from the bag, as follows:

The few in the first (central) position, relating to this world is ‡ *ur*. This few signifies passion and thus is instantly relatable to what is driving the querent.

The second few, in the Underworld position, is ‡ *idad*, signifying an ending and transformation. It is the ogham of death and rebirth. This shows that the matter is much deeper than a simple lust for this woman, and it transpires that the querent is already married.

The third few, in the Otherworld position, is ∃ *coll*, whose bright creativity signifies all manner of erotic bliss should the querent proceed with his desires and hook up with this woman.

Taken as a whole, the reading acknowledges the

34

querent's passion and informs him that if he takes action upon it, the result will be at least temporarily delightful. However, it warns him in no uncertain terms that to do so would be the death knell for his marriage: he would not 'get away with it', there would be the price to pay.

The Way of the Fifths

In Celtic cosmology, just as the cosmos is divided into three 'layers' (as utilised in the Way of Brigid), so it is divided into five horizontal directions. This horizontal pattern of manifestation is what the Way of the Fifths is based upon. In this layout, five oghams are drawn and are arranged according to the following pattern:

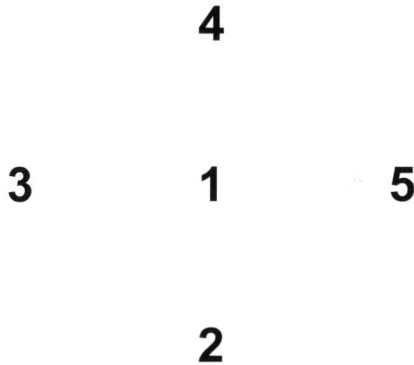

4

3   **1**   **5**

2

This represents a force which begins in the centre and then spirals around the quarters until it reaches full manifestation in the fifth position.

It will be recalled that in the chapter giving the meanings of the ogham fews, a chart was presented offering key words for each few as it appears in each of these five fields. The fields are given names in that chart and these are as follows:

Conflict

Learning   Sovereignty   Prosperity

Harmony

So the first ogham to be drawn is put in the field of Sovereignty; the second in Harmony; the third in Learning; the fourth in Conflict, and the final one in Prosperity. They are then interpreted according to their own meanings modified by the field in which they find themselves (using the key words in the chart on pages 25 and 26 as a guideline).

Example Reading Using the Way of the Fifths

In this instance, the querent has been saving money with a view to living abroad for a year. He has researched visa requirements and so forth, but wishes to know if any unforeseen elements have been overlooked and whether the move will be a positive one.

The oghams are mixed and five pulled from the bag, as follows:

>⫢

>⫼   >⟙   >⊥

>⫰

The first few, in the central field of Sovereignty, is ⊨ *luise*, which is a protective, vitalising, quickening force. Its key word in this field is **dominion**. The whole implies that the querent has made his plans well and has his life under control.

The second few, in the Southern field of Harmony, is ⊨ *fern*, which implies strong foundations and ideals. Its key word in this field is **quickness**. This suggests that the querent's objectives will be met effortlessly and without undue hassle.

The third few, in the Western field of Learning, is ≣ *cert*, which is a beautiful influence, bringing peace and a sense or timelessness. Its key word in this field is **esoterica**, implying that this experience will open the querent's eyes to previously unknown aspects of life, bringing wonder and appreciation.

The third few, in the Northern field of Conflict, is ≸ *gétal*, which signifies the crossing of borders and boundaries. This reminds the querent that leaving one's comfort zone and entering new territory is always a challenging prospect. But the key word for this few in

37

this field is **rest**, indicating that it will prove to be a liberating and relaxing experience, not a combative one.

Finally, the fifth few in the Eastern field of Prosperity, is $+$ *ailm*, which signifies a well ordered life and new beginnings, both of which are highly appropriate to the querent's plans. Its key word in this field is **originality**, foreshadowing new experiences for the querent.

The reading as a whole is completely positive, indicating a life-changing and pleasant experience.

Afterword

It is my sincere hope that this little booklet has opened your eyes to the wonders of ogham divination. It is the most direct and useful method of divination I have discovered, always offering sound practical advice.

The world of Celtic spirituality is a fascinating one, and the ogham is threaded through the world view of the western Celts. Much more information on this spiritual world, together with more layout methods and techniques for using the ogham in magical practice, are included in Michael Kelly's *The Book of Ogham*. The same author's *The Ogham Roads* offers techniques to travel through the Otherworld and Underworld in spirit vision, using the ogham as guides and signposts. Other books are suggested in the bibliography that follows.

HOW TO READ OGHAM

Bibliography

Calder, G. *Auraicept na N'Eces*. Edinburgh: John Grant, 1917.

Chadwick, Nora. *The Celts*. Harmondsworth, UK: Penguin, 1970.

Cross, Tom P. and Slover, Clark H. eds. *Ancient Irish Tales*. Dublin: Figgis, 1936. (*AIT*)

Davidson, H.R.E. *Myths and Symbols in Pagan Europe*. Syracuse: University of Syracuse Press, 1988.

Delaney, Frank. *The Celts*. Boston: Little Brown, 1986.

De Vries, Jan. *Keltische Religion*. Stuttgart: Kohlhammer, 1961.

Dooley, Ann and Roe, Harry. *Tales of the Elders of Ireland: Acallam na Sénorach*. Oxford University Press, 1999.

Eliade, Mircea. *Shamanism: Archaic Techniques of Ecstasy*. Harmondsworth, UK: Penguin, 1964.

Eluäre, Christiane. *The Celts: First Master of Europe*. New York: Thames and Hudson, 1993.

Falconar, A.E.I. *Celtic Tales of Myth and Fantasy*. Isle of Man: Non-Aristotelean Publishing, 1984.

Goodenough, Simon. *Celtic Mythology*. Twickenham, UK: Tiger Books International, 1997.

Graves, Robert. *The White Goddess*. New York: Farrar, Strauss and Girous, 1966. 2nd ed. [orig. published 1948.]

Green, Miranda. *The Gods of the Celts*. Stroud, UK: Sutton Publishing, 1986.

Hall Caine, W. Ralph. *Annals of the Magic Isle*. London: Cecil Palmer, 1926.

Kelly, Michael. *The Book of Ogham*. Isle of Man: CreateSpace,

2014.

Kelly, Michael. *The Ogham Roads*. Isle of Man: CreateSpace, 2012.

Kelly, Michael. *Words of Power*. Isle of Man: CreateSpace, 2013.

Lehmann, Ruth P. and Winfrid P. Lehmann. *An Introduction to Old Irish*. New York: The Modern Language Association, 1975.

Littleton, C.S. *The New Comparative Mythology*. Berkeley: University of California Press, 1982.

Lysaght, Patricia. *A Pocket Book of the Banshee*. Dublin: O'Brien, 1998.

Macalister, R.A. Stewart. *The Secret Languages of Ireland*. Cambridge: Cambridge University Press, 1937.

Macalister, R.A. Stewart. *Corpus inscriptionem insularum celticarum*. Dublin: Irish Manuscripts Commission, 1945.

Maccrossan, Tadhg. *The Sacred Cauldron: Secrets of the Druids*. St. Paul, MN: Llewellyn, 1991.

McManus, Damien. *Guide to Ogam*. Maynooth: An Sagart, 1991.

McManus, Damien. "Irish Letter-Names and Their Kennings." *Ériu* 37 (1988), pp. 127-168.

Matthews, Caitlin. *The Elements of the Celtic Tradition*. Longmead, UK: Element Books, 1989.

Matthews, John and Caitlin. *The Aquarian Guide to British and Irish Mythology*. Wellingborough, UK: Aquarian, 1988.

Murray, Liz and Colin. *The Celtic Tree Oracle*. London: Rider, 1988.

Patton, John-Paul. *The Poet's Ogam: A Living Magical Tradition*. Lulu, 2010.

Pennick, Nigel. *Ogham and Coelbren*. Berks, UK: Capall Bann, 2000.

Piggott, Stuart. *The Druids*. London: Thames and Hudson, 1968.

Rees, Alwyn and Brinley. *Celtic Heritage: Ancient Tradition in Ireland and Wales*. London: Thames and Hudson, 1961.

Tolstoy, Nikolai. *The Quest For Merlin*. Boston: Little Brown, 1985.

RELATED TITLES

The Book of Ogham
by Michael Kelly

A Deep Exploration of Celtic Spirituality

The Book of Ogham is a practical manual for divination using the ancient Celtic characters of ogham writing. However, it is much more than that as well. It opens the doors to the authentic understanding of ancient Celtic cosmology and psychology in ways that have never been done before. This, as much as the divinatory material, opens the reader to vistas as yet uncharted in the fields of Celtic studies.   In this book the reader will discover:

- A complete system of oghamic divination
- Four different methods of divination
- The lore of each of the 20 ogham characters
- Instructions on how to make ogham fews
- Celtic psychology
- Celtic cosmology
- A complete suggested curriculum for training in Celtic spirituality based on the ogham system

The Ogham Roads
by Michael Kelly

The Ogham Roads uses the characters of the ancient Celtic writing system to tap into mythic imagery and guide the reader on a conceptual journey through the mysterious Otherworld and Underworld realms of Celtic legend.

In so doing, the reader encounters archetypal characters and situations and engages in a deep level exploration of their own minds, coming to know themselves and their own abilities and potential as never before.

To tread The Ogham Roads is a truly life-affirming and life-changing experience.

This book uses the ogham letters and their associated myths to connect with streams of ancestral consciousness and simultaneously reach out to the future. It offers a transformative and wondrous experience for those who will put it into practice.

Printed in Great Britain
by Amazon.co.uk, Ltd.,
Marston Gate.